MAD LIBS®

By Roger Price and Leonard Stern

PSS!
PRICE STERN SLOAN

PRICE STERN SLOAN
Published by the Penguin Group
Penguin Group (USA) Inc., 375 Hudson Street, New York, New York 10014, USA
Penguin Group (Canada), 90 Eglinton Avenue East, Suite 700,
Toronto, Ontario M4P 2Y3, Canada
(a division of Pearson Penguin Canada Inc.)
Penguin Books Ltd., 80 Strand, London WC2R 0RL, England
Penguin Group Ireland, 25 St. Stephen's Green, Dublin 2, Ireland
(a division of Penguin Books Ltd.)
Penguin Group (Australia), 250 Camberwell Road, Camberwell, Victoria 3124, Australia
(a division of Pearson Australia Group Pty. Ltd.)
Penguin Books India Pvt. Ltd., 11 Community Centre,
Panchsheel Park, New Delhi—110 017, India
Penguin Group (NZ), 67 Apollo Drive, Rosedale, North Shore 0632, New Zealand
(a division of Pearson New Zealand Ltd.)
Penguin Books (South Africa) (Pty.) Ltd., 24 Sturdee Avenue,
Rosebank, Johannesburg 2196, South Africa

Penguin Books Ltd., Registered Offices:
80 Strand, London WC2R 0RL, England

Published by Price Stern Sloan,
a division of Penguin Young Readers Group,
345 Hudson Street, New York, New York 10014.

ISBN 978-0-8431-3225-0

1 3 5 7 9 10 8 6 4 2

MAD LIBS®

INSTRUCTIONS

MAD LIBS® is a game for people who don't like games!
It can be played by one, two, three, four, or forty.

● RIDICULOUSLY SIMPLE DIRECTIONS

In this tablet you will find stories containing blank spaces where words are left out. One player, the **READER**, selects one of these stories. The **READER** does not tell anyone what the story is about. Instead, he/she asks the other players, the **WRITERS**, to give him/her words. These words are used to fill in the blank spaces in the story.

● TO PLAY

The **READER** asks each **WRITER** in turn to call out words—an adjective or a noun or whatever the space calls for—and uses them to fill in the blank spaces in the story. The result is a **MAD LIBS®** game.

When the **READER** then reads the completed **MAD LIBS®** game to the other players, they will discover that they have written a story that is fantastic, screamingly funny, shocking, silly, crazy, or just plain dumb—depending upon which words each **WRITER** called out.

● EXAMPLE *(Before and After)*

" _____ !" he said _____
       EXCLAMATION   ADVERB

as he jumped into his convertible _____ and
                                                  NOUN

drove off with his _____ wife.
                                 ADJECTIVE

" *Ouch* !" he said *stupidly*
       EXCLAMATION   ADVERB

as he jumped into his convertible *cat* and
                                          NOUN

drove off with his *brave* wife.
                           ADJECTIVE

MAD LIBS®

QUICK REVIEW

In case you have forgotten what adjectives, adverbs, nouns, and verbs are, here is a quick review:

An **ADJECTIVE** describes something or somebody. *Lumpy, soft, ugly, messy,* and *short* are adjectives.

An **ADVERB** tells how something is done. It modifies a verb and usually ends in "ly." *Modestly, stupidly, greedily,* and *carefully* are adverbs.

A **NOUN** is the name of a person, place, or thing. *Sidewalk, umbrella, bridle, bathtub,* and *nose* are nouns.

A **VERB** is an action word. *Run, pitch, jump,* and *swim* are verbs. Put the verbs in past tense if the directions say PAST TENSE. *Ran, pitched, jumped,* and *swam* are verbs in the past tense.

When we ask for **A PLACE**, we mean any sort of place: a country or city *(Spain, Cleveland)* or a room *(bathroom, kitchen).*

An **EXCLAMATION** or **SILLY WORD** is any sort of funny sound, gasp, grunt, or outcry, like *Wow!, Ouch!, Whomp!, Ick!,* and *Gadzooks!*

When we ask for specific words, like a **NUMBER**, a **COLOR**, an **ANIMAL**, or a **PART OF THE BODY**, we mean a word that is one of those things, like *seven, blue, horse,* or *head.*

When we ask for a **PLURAL**, it means more than one. For example, *cat* pluralized is *cats.*

MAD LIBS® is fun to play with friends, but you can also play it by yourself! To begin with, DO NOT look at the story on the page below. Fill in the blanks on this page with the words called for. Then, using the words you have selected, fill in the blank spaces in the story.

Now you've created your own hilarious MAD LIBS® game!

THE GREATEST SHOW ON EARTH, BY HAM

OCCUPATION _____

ADJECTIVE _____

NOUN _____

ADJECTIVE _____

PLURAL NOUN _____

VERB ENDING IN "ING" _____

ADJECTIVE _____

NOUN _____

PLURAL NOUN _____

NOUN _____

NOUN _____

PLURAL NOUN _____

ARTICLE OF CLOTHING _____

ADJECTIVE _____

MAD LIBS®
QUIZ

Do you have the right _____ to be a space chimp?

NOUN

Take this _____ quiz to find out!

ADJECTIVE

1. When there is a/an _____ mission in need of a crew, you:

ADJECTIVE

   a) volunteer _____. You can't wait to serve your

ADVERB

   _____.

NOUN

   b) hide in the _____ closet.

NOUN

2. When the ship is damaged by a flying _____, you:

NOUN

   a) keep a level _____ and repair the damage.

PART OF THE BODY

   b) scream "_____!" and head for the escape _____.

EXCLAMATION   NOUN

3. When off duty, you:

   a) _____ study your *Simian Space Manual*.

ADVERB

   b) go out to a/an _____ party in (the) _____.

ADJECTIVE   A PLACE

If you answered mostly As, congratulations! Welcome aboard the

Chimpfinity. If you answered mostly Bs, you might want to consider

a career as a/an _____!

OCCUPATION

MAD LIBS® is fun to play with friends, but you can also play it by yourself! To begin with, DO NOT look at the story on the page below. Fill in the blanks on this page with the words called for. Then, using the words you have selected, fill in the blank spaces in the story.

Now you've created your own hilarious MAD LIBS® game!

CODE OF CONDUCT, BY TITAN

NOUN _____

PLURAL NOUN _____

ADVERB _____

ADJECTIVE _____

NUMBER _____

PLURAL NOUN _____

PLURAL NOUN _____

NOUN _____

ADJECTIVE _____

ADVERB _____

NOUN _____

VERB ENDING IN "ING" _____

ADJECTIVE _____

NOUN _____

NOUN _____

NOUN _____

ADJECTIVE _____

ADJECTIVE _____

MAD LIBS®

CODE OF CONDUCT, BY TITAN

There's more to being a space _____ than experiencing
                                            NOUN

antigravity _____. You've also got to obey the rules!
                PLURAL NOUN

You must always behave _____. A spaceship is a very
                            ADVERB

_____ piece of equipment that costs _____
        ADJECTIVE   NUMBER

dollars to build. It is therefore not appropriate to swing from the

_____ or throw _____ at the captain! You should
    PLURAL NOUN   PLURAL NOUN

address your superior officers as either "Sir" or "_____,"
                                                        NOUN

and never disobey a/an _____ order. When everybody
                            ADJECTIVE

follows the rules, the mission goes _____. On our mission
                                        ADVERB

to Malgor, Ham broke every rule in the _____.
                                            NOUN

He was always _____ around, acting like a/an
                VERB ENDING IN "ING"

_____ _____. But even though he's a
    ADJECTIVE   NOUN

rule-breaking _____, he's also a brave _____,
                NOUN   NOUN

and I'm proud to call him my _____ crewmate. But I
                                ADJECTIVE

wish he would stop calling me a/an _____-head!
                                        ADJECTIVE

MAD LIBS® is fun to play with friends, but you can also play it by yourself! To begin with, DO NOT look at the story on the page below. Fill in the blanks on this page with the words called for. Then, using the words you have selected, fill in the blank spaces in the story.

Now you've created your own hilarious MAD LIBS® game!

LUNA'S DREAM, BY LUNA

NOUN _____

PLURAL NOUN _____

SILLY WORD _____

OCCUPATION _____

CELEBRITY_____

SAME CELEBRITY _____

VERB _____

PLURAL NOUN _____

PLURAL NOUN _____

ADVERB _____

NOUN _____

ADVERB _____

PLURAL NOUN _____

ADJECTIVE _____

NOUN _____

PART OF THE BODY (PLURAL) _____

ADJECTIVE _____

MAD LIBS®
LUNA'S DREAM, BY LUNA

Ever since I was a little _____ playing with my
                                    NOUN

toy _____ and pretending they were aliens from
       PLURAL NOUN

Planet _____, I knew I wanted to become a space
          SILLY WORD

_____. I would look at the poster of _____
   OCCUPATION   CELEBRITY

on my wall and think, "Someday, just like _____, I'll
                                            SAME CELEBRITY

_____ into outer space and explore new _____,
   VERB   PLURAL NOUN

discover important _____, and _____
                      PLURAL NOUN   ADVERB

go where no _____ has gone before!" Determined
                NOUN

to achieve my dream, I studied _____ in school and
                                     ADVERB

got accepted to the Space _____ Academy, where I
                              PLURAL NOUN

received top honors for my _____ grades. Then, on
                               ADJECTIVE

my first outer space assignment with Ham and Titan, the spaceship

blasted out of the Earth's _____, and I couldn't believe my
                               NOUN

_____. It was official—I was a real, _____
PART OF THE BODY (PLURAL)   ADJECTIVE

space chimp!

MAD LIBS® is fun to play with friends, but you can also play it by yourself! To begin with, DO NOT look at the story on the page below. Fill in the blanks on this page with the words called for. Then, using the words you have selected, fill in the blank spaces in the story.

Now you've created your own hilarious MAD LIBS® game!

BACK IN MY DAY, BY HOUSTON

PLURAL NOUN _____

PLURAL NOUN _____

NOUN _____

NOUN _____

PART OF THE BODY _____

NOUN _____

VERB (PAST TENSE) _____

NOUN _____

TYPE OF LIQUID _____

PLURAL NOUN _____

PLURAL NOUN _____

VERB _____

PLURAL NOUN _____

ADJECTIVE _____

PLURAL NOUN _____

MAD LIBS®
BACK IN MY DAY,
BY HOUSTON

What's the matter with _____ today? Who can

PLURAL NOUN

understand all these newfangled gadgets and _____?

PLURAL NOUN

Back in my day, chimps didn't use _____-Berry phones;

NOUN

we had two cans connected by a/an _____. You talked

NOUN

into one can and then held it up to your _____

PART OF THE BODY

to listen. If the _____ on the other end couldn't hear

NOUN

you, you just _____ louder. If the string broke, then

VERB (PAST TENSE)

you just understood that that's the way the _____

NOUN

crumbles, and it was no use crying over spilled _____.

TYPE OF LIQUID

But it seldom broke, because in those days, when we made

_____, we built them to last. Not like these

PLURAL NOUN

newfangled _____ today that break if you so much

PLURAL NOUN

as _____ on them. No sir. We may not have had fancy

VERB

_____ or _____ gizmos, but we had

PLURAL NOUN   ADJECTIVE

our _____, and that was enough for us!

PLURAL NOUN

MAD LIBS® is fun to play with friends, but you can also play it by yourself! To begin with, DO NOT look at the story on the page below. Fill in the blanks on this page with the words called for. Then, using the words you have selected, fill in the blank spaces in the story.

Now you've created your own hilarious MAD LIBS® game!

TO TRAIN A CHIMP, BY HAM

ADJECTIVE _____

NOUN _____

ADVERB _____

VERB ENDING IN "ING" _____

PART OF THE BODY (PLURAL) _____

VERB _____

VERB _____

ADJECTIVE _____

VERB ENDING IN "ING" _____

ADJECTIVE _____

ADJECTIVE _____

ADJECTIVE _____

PLURAL NOUN _____

PART OF THE BODY _____

ARTICLE OF CLOTHING (PLURAL) _____

PART OF THE BODY (PLURAL) _____

ADJECTIVE _____

MAD LIBS®

TO TRAIN A CHIMP, BY HAM

One of my favorite parts of becoming a space chimp was the

_____ training program. First, they put me, Titan,
　　　ADJECTIVE

and Luna inside a giant _____ and spun it around
　　　　　　　　　　　　　NOUN

really _____ to simulate _____ in
　　　　ADVERB　　　　　　　　　　　VERB ENDING IN "ING"

the spaceship. The g-forces made our _____
　　　　　　　　　　　　　　　　　PART OF THE BODY (PLURAL)

_____. It was awesome! Then they had us _____ on
　　VERB　　　　　　　　　　　　　　　　　　　　　　VERB

treadmills, and Titan and I sang _____ songs to pass the
　　　　　　　　　　　　　　　ADJECTIVE

time. Next, they tested our _____ ability and how well
　　　　　　　　　　　VERB ENDING IN "ING"

we could remember _____ sequences on the control
　　　　　　　　　ADJECTIVE

panel—but I just used the buttons to play _____
　　　　　　　　　　　　　　　　　　　ADJECTIVE

tunes like "Let's Get _____." They also examined how
　　　　　　　　ADJECTIVE

many _____ we could eat without getting sick, though I
　　　PLURAL NOUN

don't know why. I'm still scratching my _____ over that
　　　　　　　　　　　　　　　PART OF THE BODY

one! And when it was all over, they issued us official Simian Space

_____. They make my _____
ARTICLE OF CLOTHING (PLURAL)　　　　　PART OF THE BODY (PLURAL)

look really _____, if I do say so myself!
　　　　ADJECTIVE

FROM SPACE CHIMPS™ MAD LIBS® • Space Chimps TM & © 2008 Vanguard Animation, LLC.
All Rights Reserved. Published by Price Stern Sloan, a division of Penguin Young Readers Group,
345 Hudson Street, New York, NY 10014.

MAD LIBS® is fun to play with friends, but you can also play it by yourself! To begin with, DO NOT look at the story on the page below. Fill in the blanks on this page with the words called for. Then, using the words you have selected, fill in the blank spaces in the story.

Now you've created your own hilarious MAD LIBS® game!

A TOUR OF THE CHIMPFINITY, BY HAM

ADJECTIVE _____

PLURAL NOUN _____

NOUN _____

ADVERB _____

VERB _____

NOUN _____

NOUN _____

NOUN _____

ADJECTIVE _____

ADJECTIVE _____

PART OF THE BODY _____

VERB _____

NOUN _____

ADJECTIVE _____

TYPE OF LIQUID _____

PLURAL NOUN _____

NOUN _____

MAD LIBS®
A TOUR OF THE *CHIMPFINITY*, BY HAM

Hey, guys—come check out the _____ *Chimpfinity*! It's the

ADJECTIVE

coolest ship, decked out with all the bells and _____.

PLURAL NOUN

This is the _____-pit, where we control how _____

NOUN   ADVERB

the ship will _____. Here's the captain's chair, on which

VERB

I am now placing a whoopee _____. Don't tell Titan. And

NOUN

over here we have the control _____—the heart and

NOUN

_____ of this _____ ship. Through

NOUN   ADJECTIVE

that door is the sick bay. Got a/an _____ headache?

ADJECTIVE

Twisted your _____? You can just go in there and

PART OF THE BODY

_____ it off. Downstairs is the supply _____,

VERB   NOUN

where we keep the _____ canisters of _____

ADJECTIVE   TYPE OF LIQUID

that fuel the ship. As you can see, the *Chimpfinity* has all the

_____ a/an _____ could want in outer space!

PLURAL NOUN   NOUN

FROM SPACE CHIMPS™ MAD LIBS® • Space Chimps TM & © 2008 Vanguard Animation, LLC.
All Rights Reserved. Published by Price Stern Sloan, a division of Penguin Young Readers Group,
345 Hudson Street, New York, NY 10014.

MAD LIBS® is fun to play with friends, but you can also play it by yourself! To begin with, DO NOT look at the story on the page below. Fill in the blanks on this page with the words called for. Then, using the words you have selected, fill in the blank spaces in the story.

Now you've created your own hilarious MAD LIBS® game!

BRAINIACS

NOUN _____

SAME NOUN _____

ADJECTIVE _____

ADJECTIVE _____

PLURAL NOUN _____

NOUN _____

SILLY WORD _____

NOUN _____

VERB ENDING IN "ING" _____

ADVERB _____

NOUN _____

SAME NOUN _____

SAME NOUN _____

VERB _____

PLURAL NOUN _____

ADJECTIVE _____

ADJECTIVE _____

NOUN _____

MAD LIBS
BRAINIACS

Dr. Poole, Dr. Bob, and Dr. Jagu (with some help from Houston)

explain how a/an _____ is launched into space:
<small>NOUN</small>

Dr. Poole: Launching a/an _____ is a very _____
<small>SAME NOUN</small>   <small>ADJECTIVE</small>

process. An astronaut (or chimp) presses a/an _____
<small>ADJECTIVE</small>

button on the control panel, generating _____
<small>PLURAL NOUN</small>

that rotate the _____.
<small>NOUN</small>

Dr. Bob: This sends a signal to the _____ accelerator,
<small>SILLY WORD</small>

which causes the ship's _____ to start _____.
<small>NOUN</small>   <small>VERB ENDING IN "ING"</small>

Dr. Jagu: Then the countdown starts, and you have to be sure to count

_____, saying, "Ten _____, nine _____, eight
<small>ADVERB</small>   <small>NOUN</small>   <small>SAME NOUN</small>

_____ . . ." When you reach one, you say, "_____
<small>SAME NOUN</small>   <small>VERB</small>

off!" Then thousands of tiny _____ explode from
<small>PLURAL NOUN</small>

the engines, creating the _____ thrust that sends
<small>ADJECTIVE</small>

the _____ ship up, up, and away!
<small>ADJECTIVE</small>

Houston: So simple, a/an _____ could do it!
<small>NOUN</small>

FROM SPACE CHIMPS™ MAD LIBS® • Space Chimps TM & © 2008 Vanguard Animation, LLC.
All Rights Reserved. Published by Price Stern Sloan, a division of Penguin Young Readers Group,
345 Hudson Street, New York, NY 10014.

MAD LIBS® is fun to play with friends, but you can also play it by yourself! To begin with, DO NOT look at the story on the page below. Fill in the blanks on this page with the words called for. Then, using the words you have selected, fill in the blank spaces in the story.

Now you've created your own hilarious MAD LIBS® game!

PLANET MALGOR, BY KILOWATT

SILLY WORD _____

SILLY WORD _____

TYPE OF LIQUID _____

ADJECTIVE _____

PLURAL NOUN _____

ADJECTIVE _____

VERB ENDING IN "ING" _____

PLURAL NOUN _____

PLURAL NOUN _____

NOUN _____

ADJECTIVE _____

PERSON IN ROOM _____

A PLACE _____

VERB _____

ADJECTIVE _____

VERB _____

NOUN _____

MAD LIBS®
PLANET MALGOR,
BY KILOWATT

The planet Malgor is located in the _____ quadrant
SILLY WORD

of the _____ galaxy. It is known for its abundance of
SILLY WORD

_____ and its _____ life-forms. Most
TYPE OF LIQUID   ADJECTIVE

of Malgor's inhabitants are fun-loving _____. They have
PLURAL NOUN

a/an _____ annual Snizzlefruit Frolic Festival, where
ADJECTIVE

everyone gets together for a day of nonstop _____! And
VERB ENDING IN "ING"

Malgorians love to drink Lemonslort, which tastes like squeezed

_____ and sugar. Yum! But beware—Malgor is not
PLURAL NOUN

all fun and _____. You must watch out for the Cave of
PLURAL NOUN

the _____-Devouring Beast and the Valley of Very
NOUN

_____ Things. Very scary! But if you meet a member
ADJECTIVE

of the Luzian species, like me, you'll be in luck. Just say, "Hi! I'm

_____! I'm from (the) _____, and I've come
PERSON IN ROOM   A PLACE

to Malgor to _____," and you will have made a/an
VERB

_____ friend for life. You may even decide to
ADJECTIVE

_____ here for the rest of your _____!
VERB   NOUN

FROM SPACE CHIMPS™ MAD LIBS® • Space Chimps TM & © 2008 Vanguard Animation, LLC.
All Rights Reserved. Published by Price Stern Sloan, a division of Penguin Young Readers Group,
345 Hudson Street, New York, NY 10014.

MAD LIBS® is fun to play with friends, but you can also play it by yourself! To begin with, DO NOT look at the story on the page below. Fill in the blanks on this page with the words called for. Then, using the words you have selected, fill in the blank spaces in the story.

Now you've created your own hilarious MAD LIBS® game!

COMMANDER'S SPACE LOG, BY TITAN

NUMBER _____

NOUN _____

ADJECTIVE _____

ADJECTIVE _____

NOUN _____

ADJECTIVE _____

CELEBRITY_____

NOUN _____

ADJECTIVE _____

VERB _____

ADVERB _____

TYPE OF LIQUID _____

ADJECTIVE _____

ADJECTIVE _____

PLURAL NOUN _____

MAD LIBS®
COMMANDER'S SPACE LOG, BY TITAN

Commander's Space Log: star date six point _____
NUMBER

_____ alpha. After our spaceship crash-landed thanks
NOUN

to Ham's _____ job performance, I awoke to find
ADJECTIVE

myself all alone on the spaceship. I heard _____
ADJECTIVE

voices outside and peeked through a window to discover dozens

of little _____-like creatures surrounding my ship.
NOUN

It seems they are ruled by a/an _____ creature who
ADJECTIVE

calls himself Zartog and looks a bit like _____, only
CELEBRITY

with sharper cheekbones. He uses a/an _____ to
NOUN

terrify the smaller _____ creatures. Whenever they
ADJECTIVE

_____, he _____ dips them into a vat
VERB   ADVERB

of _____, and they become _____
TYPE OF LIQUID   ADJECTIVE

statues. I will attempt to make _____ contact with these
ADJECTIVE

beings. Hopefully, they will greet me with open _____.
PLURAL NOUN

FROM SPACE CHIMPS™ MAD LIBS® • Space Chimps TM & © 2008 Vanguard Animation, LLC.
All Rights Reserved. Published by Price Stern Sloan, a division of Penguin Young Readers Group,
345 Hudson Street, New York, NY 10014.

MAD LIBS® is fun to play with friends, but you can also play it by yourself! To begin with, DO NOT look at the story on the page below. Fill in the blanks on this page with the words called for. Then, using the words you have selected, fill in the blank spaces in the story.

Now you've created your own hilarious MAD LIBS® game!

IF I WERE KING, BY ZARTOG

NOUN _____

SILLY WORD _____

ADJECTIVE _____

NOUN _____

ADJECTIVE _____

PLURAL NOUN _____

ADJECTIVE _____

A PLACE _____

TYPE OF LIQUID _____

VERB ENDING IN "ING" _____

NOUN _____

PART OF THE BODY _____

VERB ENDING IN "ING" _____

VERB ENDING IN "ING" _____

NOUN _____

ADJECTIVE _____

PLURAL NOUN _____

MAD LIBS®
IF I WERE KING, BY ZARTOG

If I were the royal _____ of Malgor, I would eat
NOUN

snizzlefruit and _____ treats all day long. I'd throw
SILLY WORD

_____ parties and have everyone bow down before
ADJECTIVE

my _____. I would build a/an _____
NOUN   ADJECTIVE

palace and decorate it with solid-gold _____—just like
PLURAL NOUN

that famous _____ palace in (the) _____. I'd spend
ADJECTIVE   A PLACE

my afternoons dipping traitors into a pool of _____
TYPE OF LIQUID

and putting them on display in my _____ room. My
VERB ENDING IN "ING"

clothes would be made of real _____-skin, and I
NOUN

would never have to lift a/an _____ to do work ever
PART OF THE BODY

again. Nevermore would my _____ be interrupted
VERB ENDING IN "ING"

by the sounds of children _____. Nevermore would
VERB ENDING IN "ING"

I have to endure the villagers' annual Snizzle-_____
NOUN

Frolic Festival. If I were king, there would be only one festival, and it

would be to honor my _____ _____!
ADJECTIVE   PLURAL NOUN

MAD LIBS® is fun to play with friends, but you can also play it by yourself! To begin with, DO NOT look at the story on the page below. Fill in the blanks on this page with the words called for. Then, using the words you have selected, fill in the blank spaces in the story.

Now you've created your own hilarious MAD LIBS® game!

FIRST DATE, BY HAM

ADJECTIVE _____

PART OF THE BODY (PLURAL) _____

A PLACE _____

NUMBER _____

PLURAL NOUN _____

VERB ENDING IN "ING" _____

PLURAL NOUN _____

PLURAL NOUN _____

ADJECTIVE _____

NOUN _____

ADJECTIVE _____

NOUN _____

SILLY WORD _____

ADJECTIVE _____

MAD LIBS®
FIRST DATE, BY HAM

One day, Luna and I will tell our grandchimps the _____

ADJECTIVE

story of the day we fell head over _____ for each

PART OF THE BODY (PLURAL)

other. We had just crash-landed on (the) _____ when

A PLACE

Luna and I decided to investigate our surroundings. Suddenly,

_____-foot-tall snakes emerged from beneath some

NUMBER

_____! We dodged them only to face the

PLURAL NOUN

_____ fluvian fighters, who threw _____ at

VERB ENDING IN "ING" PLURAL NOUN

us. Then we swung through a jungle on vines that were actually

chimp-eating _____! Next, we fell down a/an _____

PLURAL NOUN ADJECTIVE

canyon, where Luna landed on a soft _____, and I

NOUN

performed one of my famous crash landings. Finally, we made our

way through the Valley of Very _____ Things, the Cave

ADJECTIVE

of the _____-Devouring Beast, and the Dark Cloud

NOUN

of _____, and then—*voilà*! We saved the _____

SILLY WORD ADJECTIVE

planet and came home. Pretty exciting for a first date!

FROM SPACE CHIMPS™ MAD LIBS® • Space Chimps TM & © 2008 Vanguard Animation, LLC.
All Rights Reserved. Published by Price Stern Sloan, a division of Penguin Young Readers Group,
345 Hudson Street, New York, NY 10014.

MAD LIBS® is fun to play with friends, but you can also play it by yourself! To begin with, DO NOT look at the story on the page below. Fill in the blanks on this page with the words called for. Then, using the words you have selected, fill in the blank spaces in the story.

Now you've created your own hilarious MAD LIBS® game!

HOW TO BE BRAVE,
BY KILOWATT

ADJECTIVE _____

ADJECTIVE _____

ADVERB _____

PART OF THE BODY _____

ADJECTIVE _____

ADJECTIVE _____

ADJECTIVE _____

PART OF THE BODY (PLURAL) _____

PLURAL NOUN _____

ADJECTIVE _____

VERB _____

ADJECTIVE _____

PLURAL NOUN _____

PART OF THE BODY (PLURAL) _____

NUMBER _____

MAD LIBS®
HOW TO BE BRAVE,
BY KILOWATT

I've been scared of many _____ things throughout
ADJECTIVE

my _____ life. And it's _____ obvious
ADJECTIVE   ADVERB

when I'm scared, because my _____ lights up! But
PART OF THE BODY

then one _____ day I met a chimp named Ham, and
ADJECTIVE

he gave me some _____ advice. He said to imagine
ADJECTIVE

what I'm most afraid of and to picture myself overcoming this

_____ fear. From that moment on, whenever I'm
ADJECTIVE

scared, I close my _____ and imagine myself
PART OF THE BODY (PLURAL)

alone in a room full of evil _____. I surprise my
PLURAL NOUN

enemies with _____ karate moves. I chop! I kick! I
ADJECTIVE

_____! Awed by my _____ skills, they run
VERB   ADJECTIVE

for their _____. Then I open my _____,
PLURAL NOUN   PART OF THE BODY (PLURAL)

and I feel much braver! It's as easy as one, two, _____!
NUMBER

MAD LIBS® is fun to play with friends, but you can also play it by yourself! To begin with, DO NOT look at the story on the page below. Fill in the blanks on this page with the words called for. Then, using the words you have selected, fill in the blank spaces in the story.

Now you've created your own hilarious MAD LIBS® game!

ANOTHER VISIT TO THE DARK CLOUD OF ID, BY HAM

NOUN _____

PLURAL NOUN _____

ARTICLE OF CLOTHING (PLURAL) _____

PLURAL NOUN _____

OCCUPATION _____

PLURAL NOUN _____

NOUN _____

NOUN _____

ADJECTIVE _____

PART OF THE BODY (PLURAL) _____

ADVERB _____

NOUN _____

NOUN _____

I can't explain it, Doc. I keep having this dream that I'm a giant

_____ being chased by a whole bunch of little
NOUN

_____. And then I turn a corner and realize I'm not
PLURAL NOUN

wearing any _____! Suddenly, I find myself
ARTICLE OF CLOTHING (PLURAL)

onstage in front of hundreds of _____, and I'm about
PLURAL NOUN

to perform a speech from Shakespeare's *The* _____
OCCUPATION

of Venice when I realize I've forgotten all my _____!
PLURAL NOUN

What can it mean? I'm sure it all goes back to my childhood. On my

third birthday, I really wanted a/an _____, but my
NOUN

parents got me a/an _____ instead. I've been a/an
NOUN

_____ mess ever since. Maybe I just need to close my
ADJECTIVE

_____, breathe _____, and try to
PART OF THE BODY (PLURAL)   ADVERB

find my happy _____. What do you think, Doc? Am I a
NOUN

hopeless _____, or can you fix me?
NOUN

FROM SPACE CHIMPS™ MAD LIBS® • Space Chimps TM & © 2008 Vanguard Animation, LLC.
All Rights Reserved. Published by Price Stern Sloan, a division of Penguin Young Readers Group,
345 Hudson Street, New York, NY 10014.

MAD LIBS® is fun to play with friends, but you can also play it by yourself! To begin with, DO NOT look at the story on the page below. Fill in the blanks on this page with the words called for. Then, using the words you have selected, fill in the blank spaces in the story.

Now you've created your own hilarious MAD LIBS® game!

COMET TO THE RESCUE

VERB _____

ADJECTIVE _____

NOUN _____

ADVERB _____

NOUN _____

NUMBER _____

PLURAL NOUN _____

ADJECTIVE _____

NOUN _____

ADJECTIVE _____

ADJECTIVE _____

ADVERB _____

NOUN _____

EXCLAMATION _____

VERB ENDING IN "ING"_____

PLURAL NOUN _____

MAD LIBS
COMET TO THE RESCUE

When I found out that I wasn't going to _____ with Ham,
                                          VERB

Luna, and Titan on the mission to Malgor, I felt pretty _____.
                                                         ADJECTIVE

But I still got to play an important _____. Their spaceship
                                      NOUN

flew back to Earth without them, and they were _____
                                                 ADVERB

stranded. Luckily, I had made them a banana _____ so
                                             NOUN

they could talk to me from _____ miles away. But time was
                            NUMBER

short. The _____ in the sky were about to line up,
            PLURAL NOUN

which would trigger a/an _____ volcanic eruption. I told
                         ADJECTIVE

them that they had to turn their probe into a/an _____
                                                  NOUN

and blast off out of the _____ volcano. I helped them
                          ADJECTIVE

reengineer the probe's _____ structure and attach a
                        ADJECTIVE

nose cone so they could _____ reenter Earth's atmosphere.
                         ADVERB

They put the probe in the _____'s crater, and when
                           NOUN

the volcano erupted—_____!—they were
                       EXCLAMATION

_____ through the universe toward home. It just goes
VERB ENDING IN "ING"

to show that even small chimps can make big _____!
                                             PLURAL NOUN

MAD LIBS® is fun to play with friends, but you can also play it by yourself! To begin with, DO NOT look at the story on the page below. Fill in the blanks on this page with the words called for. Then, using the words you have selected, fill in the blank spaces in the story.

Now you've created your own hilarious MAD LIBS® game!

TEAMWORK, BY HAM

VERB ENDING IN "ING" _____

VERB ENDING IN "ING" _____

ADJECTIVE _____

VERB _____

NOUN _____

VERB (PAST TENSE) _____

PLURAL NOUN _____

A PLACE _____

NOUN _____

PART OF THE BODY (PLURAL) _____

ADVERB _____

PLURAL NOUN _____

SAME PLURAL NOUN _____

PLURAL NOUN _____

ADVERB _____

ADJECTIVE _____

NOUN _____

ADJECTIVE _____

ADJECTIVE _____

MAD LIBS®
TEAMWORK, BY HAM

_____ together is better than _____
VERB ENDING IN "ING"   VERB ENDING IN "ING"

alone. Luna, Titan, and I would not have made it home were it not

for _____ teamwork. Everyone pitched in. Comet told
ADJECTIVE

us how to _____ through the banana _____,
VERB   NOUN

while Houston _____. The fluvians lifted and carried
VERB (PAST TENSE)

metal _____ from (the) _____ all the way
PLURAL NOUN   A PLACE

over to the launch _____. Kilowatt and the other Luzians
NOUN

used their _____ to provide light to work by. Titan
PART OF THE BODY (PLURAL)

_____ lifted heavy _____ and then
ADVERB   PLURAL NOUN

the globhoppers, by mimicking him, were able to lift some heavy

_____, too. Some alien children helped us secure
SAME PLURAL NOUN

metal _____ to the outside of the ship so it would fly more
PLURAL NOUN

_____. In the end, we built a ship that could rival any
ADVERB

_____ _____. And we made it home safe and
ADJECTIVE   NOUN

_____, thanks to our _____ friends!
ADJECTIVE   ADJECTIVE

MAD LIBS® is fun to play with friends, but you can also play it by yourself! To begin with, DO NOT look at the story on the page below. Fill in the blanks on this page with the words called for. Then, using the words you have selected, fill in the blank spaces in the story.

Now you've created your own hilarious MAD LIBS® game!

LESSONS LEARNED, BY HAM

NOUN _____

PLURAL NOUN _____

ADJECTIVE _____

PLURAL NOUN _____

VERB _____

PLURAL NOUN _____

LETTER OF THE ALPHABET _____

VERB _____

TYPE OF LIQUID _____

ADJECTIVE _____

ADJECTIVE _____

ADJECTIVE _____

VERB _____

ADJECTIVE _____

MAD LIBS®
LESSONS LEARNED, BY HAM

My first journey as a space _____ changed my whole
                                        NOUN

outlook on _____. I've learned many _____
          PLURAL NOUN   ADJECTIVE

life lessons, such as:

- Life isn't all fun and _____. Sometimes you have to
                           PLURAL NOUN

  _____ hard.
      VERB

- You can accomplish anything if you just believe in your

  _____.
    PLURAL NOUN

- There is no _____ in *team*.
        LETTER OF THE ALPHABET

- Live together, _____ alone.
          VERB

- When life gives you lemons, make _____.
                      TYPE OF LIQUID

- When the going gets tough, the _____ get going.
                    ADJECTIVE

Oh, and the most _____ thing I've learned on my
            ADJECTIVE

journey? If you want to have a really _____ party,
                      ADJECTIVE

invite some globhoppers. They really know how to _____
                      VERB

a rug. I should know—I taught them all their _____
                    ADJECTIVE

moves!

FROM SPACE CHIMPS™ MAD LIBS® • Space Chimps TM & © 2008 Vanguard Animation, LLC.
All Rights Reserved. Published by Price Stern Sloan, a division of Penguin Young Readers Group,
345 Hudson Street, New York, NY 10014.

MAD LIBS® is fun to play with friends, but you can also play it by yourself! To begin with, DO NOT look at the story on the page below. Fill in the blanks on this page with the words called for. Then, using the words you have selected, fill in the blank spaces in the story.

Now you've created your own hilarious MAD LIBS® game!

CAMPAIGN SPEECH, BY THE SENATOR

ADJECTIVE _____

PLURAL NOUN _____

ADJECTIVE _____

A PLACE _____

NOUN _____

PERSON IN ROOM _____

ADVERB _____

NOUN _____

ADJECTIVE _____

PLURAL NOUN _____

ADJECTIVE _____

ADJECTIVE _____

PART OF THE BODY _____

PART OF THE BODY _____

ADJECTIVE _____

ADJECTIVE _____

PLURAL NOUN _____

MAD LIBS
CAMPAIGN SPEECH, BY THE SENATOR

Ladies and gentlemen, it is a privilege to address such a/an

_____-looking group of _____. Thank you
   ADJECTIVE   PLURAL NOUN

for your support in my _____ presidential campaign. I
                     ADJECTIVE

would like to take this opportunity to remind the people of (the)

_____ that it was I who saved the _____
   A PLACE   NOUN

program. My opponent, _____, says I wanted to shut
                     PERSON IN ROOM

it down, but that is _____ preposterous! I helped
                  ADVERB

build a new _____ station, dedicated to the study of
           NOUN

_____ space, where we train both chimps and
   ADJECTIVE

_____ to be astronauts. As president, I will fund more
  PLURAL NOUN

_____ programs like this. I also want to warn you
  ADJECTIVE

against my _____ opponent. He/she has been caught
         ADJECTIVE

with his/her _____ in the cookie jar more than once.
      PART OF THE BODY

I, on the other _____, promise you _____
         PART OF THE BODY   ADJECTIVE

government, a/an _____ space program, and free pocket
         ADJECTIVE

protectors for _____ everywhere!
     PLURAL NOUN

MAD LIBS® is fun to play with friends, but you can also play it by yourself! To begin with, DO NOT look at the story on the page below. Fill in the blanks on this page with the words called for. Then, using the words you have selected, fill in the blank spaces in the story.

Now you've created your own hilarious MAD LIBS® game!

CHIMPS' NIGHT OUT

ADJECTIVE _____

PLURAL NOUN _____

ADJECTIVE _____

PLURAL NOUN _____

PLURAL NOUN _____

NOUN _____

VERB _____

ADJECTIVE _____

NOUN _____

ADJECTIVE _____

ADJECTIVE _____

NOUN _____

MAD LIBS
CHIMPS' NIGHT OUT

A snippet of _____ conversation from one of Ham
ADJECTIVE

and Luna's dates:

Luna: Thank you for taking me out to the observatory to see the

_____ tonight. I've had a/an _____ time.
PLURAL NOUN   ADJECTIVE

Ham: Did I ever tell you that you have beautiful _____?
PLURAL NOUN

Luna: Aw, I'm sure you say that to all the _____.
PLURAL NOUN

Ham: Not at all, my little snizzle-_____!
NOUN

Luna: Well, I really should be going. It's getting late, and I have to

_____ early in the morning.
VERB

Ham: But the night is _____ and so are we! Why not just
ADJECTIVE

stay out a little while longer? I'll show you my _____
NOUN

collection!

Luna: That sounds _____, but I can't. I'll see you soon, Ham.
ADJECTIVE

Ham: I'll wait with _____ breath! Until then, my little
ADJECTIVE

simian _____, au revoir!
NOUN

FROM SPACE CHIMPS™ MAD LIBS® • Space Chimps TM & © 2008 Vanguard Animation, LLC.
All Rights Reserved. Published by Price Stern Sloan, a division of Penguin Young Readers Group,
345 Hudson Street, New York, NY 10014.

MAD LIBS® is fun to play with friends, but you can also play it by yourself! To begin with, DO NOT look at the story on the page below. Fill in the blanks on this page with the words called for. Then, using the words you have selected, fill in the blank spaces in the story.

Now you've created your own hilarious MAD LIBS® game!

MAN OR MONKEY, BY DR. BOB

ADJECTIVE _____

ADJECTIVE _____

PART OF THE BODY (PLURAL) _____

SILLY WORD _____

ADJECTIVE _____

VERB ENDING IN "ING" _____

NUMBER _____

NOUN _____

VERB _____

VERB _____

ADJECTIVE _____

ADVERB _____

VERB _____

VERB (PAST TENSE) _____

MAD LIBS
MAN OR MONKEY,
BY DR. BOB

Dr. Poole, Dr. Jagu, and I would like to present some ＿＿＿＿＿＿＿＿
    ADJECTIVE

facts regarding the differences between humans and chimps. First,

both man and chimp are ＿＿＿＿＿＿＿＿＿＿ primates. Both have
                        ADJECTIVE

opposable ＿＿＿＿＿＿＿＿＿＿, but humans belong to the *Homo*
          PART OF THE BODY (PLURAL)

sapiens species, while chimps belong to the ＿＿＿＿＿＿＿ species.
                                              SILLY WORD

When we studied humans and chimps in a/an ＿＿＿＿＿＿＿＿＿＿
                                           ADJECTIVE

environment and tested their ＿＿＿＿＿＿＿＿＿＿ abilities, the
                              VERB ENDING IN "ING"

chimps outperformed the humans ＿＿＿＿＿＿＿＿＿＿ to one. We
                                NUMBER

also observed that when faced with a threatening ＿＿＿＿＿＿＿,
                                                  NOUN

humans tend to ＿＿＿＿＿＿＿＿＿＿ away, while chimps tend to
                VERB

stay and ＿＿＿＿＿＿＿＿＿＿. However, when human males were
          VERB

introduced to human females during a/an ＿＿＿＿＿＿＿＿＿＿
                                         ADJECTIVE

experiment, they smiled ＿＿＿＿＿＿＿＿＿＿, lost their ability to
                         ADVERB

＿＿＿＿＿＿＿＿＿＿, and ＿＿＿＿＿＿＿＿＿＿ around the room
    VERB   VERB (PAST TENSE)

like chimps!